Grammar Plus!
Activities to Teach and Reinforce (

Sentence Structure & Usage
Grades 4–6

Reinforcing basic grammar skills has never been easier or more fun than with this collection of intermediate-level activities. Whether you're planning for individual students, pairs, or groups, these exciting activities and reproducibles will score big with your students and make planning a cinch. Inside you'll find

- sections on these important skill areas: sentence parts, kinds of sentences and their functions, sentence structures, sentence errors, subject-verb agreement in sentences, and word usage skills
- fresh, new, and practical ideas that are designed especially for the busy teacher
- ready-to-use reproducibles

Editors:
Becky Andrews
Kim T. Griswell
Cindy Mondello

Writers:
Becky Andrews, Colleen Dabney, Michael Foster, Beth Gress,
Stephanie Willett-Smith

Art Coordinator:
Barry Slate

Artists:
Teresa R. Davidson, Theresa Lewis Goode, Susan Hodnett, Sheila Krill,
Rob Mayworth, Greg D. Rieves

Cover Artist:
Nick Greenwood

www.themailbox.com

©2000 by THE EDUCATION CENTER, INC.
All rights reserved.
ISBN #1-56234-413-7

Manufactured in the United States
10 9 8 7 6 5 4 3 2 1

Table of Contents

Sentence Parts

A *sentence* is a group of words that expresses a complete thought. The subject, the predicate, the simple subject, and the simple predicate are parts of a sentence. Other sentence parts include compound subjects, compound predicates, clauses, and phrases.

- A sentence has a subject and a predicate.
  - The subject tells what the sentence is about. It is either a noun, pronoun, or noun phrase.

  EXAMPLES **The cat** jumped from the porch.
  James is a great piano player.

  - The predicate of a sentence tells what the subject does, did, is, or was.

  EXAMPLES The cat **jumped from the porch.**
  James **is a great piano player.**

  - The simple subject is the main noun or pronoun that tells what or who the sentence is about. Usually the simple subject is just one word.

  EXAMPLE That red **dress** is so beautiful.

  - The simple predicate is the verb in the complete predicate. It can be more than one word in length.

  EXAMPLES Megan **drew** a great picture of her house.
  Our teacher **has been reading** a terrific book to us.

  - A compound subject is made up of two or more simple subjects.

  EXAMPLES **Kia and Sydney** went surfing Friday.
  Apples, oranges, and pears are half-price.

  - A compound predicate is made up of two or more simple predicates.

  EXAMPLE Sue **danced a jig and sang** a song in our musical.

- A **clause** is a group of words that has a subject and a predicate.
  — A main clause (also called a *principal* or an *independent* clause) can stand alone as a complete sentence.

  EXAMPLE   **Mom cleaned out the attic** because she wants to have a yard sale.

  — A **subordinate clause** (also called a *dependent* clause) gives an idea that is related to the main clause. It cannot stand alone as a sentence.

  EXAMPLE   Mom cleaned out the attic **because she wants to have a yard sale.**

- A **phrase** is a group of words that doesn't include a subject or predicate. Because a phrase isn't a complete thought, it is not a sentence. A phrase is used as a single part of speech. A phrase may be used as a noun, verb, adjective, or adverb. Some special types of phrases include appositives, gerund phrases, infinitive phrases, and prepositional phrases.

  — An **appositive** is a noun or noun phrase that follows another noun or noun phrase to give more information or explain it. An appositive is separated from the rest of the sentence by one or two commas.

  EXAMPLES   Our principal, **Mrs. Grice,** gave a speech today.
  That postcard is from Lima, **the capital of Peru.**

  — A **gerund phrase** is a group of words that includes a gerund. A gerund is a verb form that ends in *-ing* and is used as a noun.

  EXAMPLES   **Her going to the party** is fine with me.
  Running is my favorite activity.

  — An **infinitive phrase** includes an **infinitive** (a verb that is preceded by *to*) and any words that modify it (adverbs) or complete its meaning.

  EXAMPLES   Billy wanted **to play football.**
  I tried **to sing well.**

  — A **prepositional phrase** is a group of words that begins with a preposition and includes a noun or pronoun.

  EXAMPLES   She gave her book **to them.**
  We rode our bikes **around the neighborhood.**

Having a Ball!

Identifying subjects and predicates

Spike Michaels dunked the ball in the last three seconds of the game.

Follow the bouncing ball to this activity that helps students recognize subjects and predicates! Divide the class into groups; then give each group a highlighter and the sports section of a newspaper. Direct each student to scan the paper, highlight examples of vivid action verbs, and copy the verbs on his paper. Then have him write each verb on a construction paper cutout of a ball (such as a football or basketball). Post the cutouts on a board titled "Great Grammar's a Ball!"

Next, give each student three strips of paper. Have him label each strip with a sentence that uses one of the board's verbs. After students have written their names on the backs of their strips, have each child swap sentences with a partner. Instruct each student to draw one line under the subject and two lines under the predicate of each of his partner's sentences. When everyone is finished, direct students to return the sentences to their owners and check each other's work. Repeat this activity later when you want students to practice identifying simple subjects or simple predicates.

Keep It Simple!

Identifying simple subjects and simple predicates

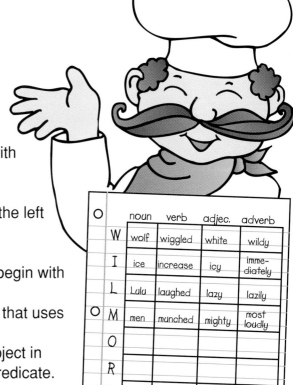

Serve up some simply sensational sentence practice with this easy-to-do activity on identifying simple subjects and predicates. Have each student follow these steps:

1. Write the name of your school (or city or state) down the left margin of a sheet of notebook paper.
2. Draw and label a chart as shown.
3. Fill in the chart with words that fit the categories and begin with the letters used in your school's name.
4. Turn your paper over. For each row, write a sentence that uses the four words in that row.
5. Swap papers with a partner. Underline the simple subject in each of your partner's sentences. Circle the simple predicate.
6. Return your partner's paper to him or her. Check to see that your partner correctly identified the simple subjects and predicates in your sentences.

Adapt this activity to practice other sentence skills, such as writing sentences with different functions (see pages 15–16).

		noun	verb	adjec.	adverb
O					
	W	wolf	wiggled	white	wildy
	I	ice	increase	icy	imme-diately
	L	Lulu	laughed	lazy	lazily
O	M	men	munched	mighty	most loudly
	O				
	R				
	E				
O					

Compound It!

Skill

Identifying compound subjects and predicates

Put this game on your menu to cook up a little practice with compound subjects and predicates! After introducing or reviewing compound subjects and predicates, divide students into small groups. Instruct each group to write ten sentences (none containing compound subjects or predicates) on a sheet of paper, skipping a line after each sentence. Then have each group cut apart its sentences and place them inside a paper bag.

To play the game, give each group a die and have students follow these steps:
1. In turn, draw a strip from the bag and read the sentence aloud.
2. Roll the die. Then change the sentence by adding a compound subject or predicate that includes the same number of nouns or verbs as the number rolled. For example, if the sentence drawn is "Potatoes are on sale at the store" and you roll a three, you might change the sentence to "Potatoes, onions, and carrots are on sale at the store." If you roll a one, you lose your turn and must return the sentence to the bag.
3. If the group agrees that your sentence is correct, you earn the number of points rolled. Return the sentence to the bag.
4. If the sentence is incorrect, the next player either tries to correct the sentence (and earns the points the previous player rolled if correct) or draws a new sentence and rerolls the die.
5. Play continues until time is up. The player with the most points wins.

Silly Sentence Wheels

Skill

Writing sentences with main and subordinate clauses

If your students think a clause is one of Kris Kringle's relatives, set them straight with this creative activity! After a lesson on main and subordinate clauses, give each pair of students one nine-inch and one six-inch construction paper circle, a ruler, a marker, and a brad. Have the students divide each circle into eight sections and then attach the smaller one atop the larger one using the brad as shown. Next, have each twosome write eight sentences that include main and subordinate clauses. Have the students underline each main clause and circle each subordinate clause. Then collect the wheels and papers and check the sentences for accuracy.

The next day, return the sentences and wheels to students. After students have corrected any errors, direct each pair to label its wheel's outer sections with its main clauses and the inner sections with its subordinate clauses. Then let the twosomes swap wheels and spin to create five silly sentences. Provide time for students to share their sentences with the class.

Positive Appositives

Using appositives

Season a lesson on appositives with this self-esteem-boosting activity! After introducing or reviewing the use of appositives in sentences, have each student write a sentence about herself that begins with her name, such as "Becca likes to play basketball." Collect the papers; then redistribute them so that no student receives her own paper. Next, instruct each child to rewrite the sentence on her paper by inserting an appositive that explains, identifies, or renames (in a positive way) the sentence's subject. For example: *Becca, an excellent soccer player, likes to play basketball.* After everyone is finished, have each student trade papers and add another sentence that includes an appositive to the paper. Continue trading until each paper includes five (or more) sentences. Then return the papers to their owners and let each child share her favorite sentence with the class.

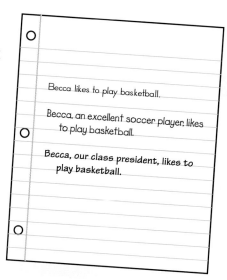

Becca likes to play basketball.

Becca, an excellent soccer player, likes to play basketball.

Becca, our class president, likes to play basketball.

Your left hand is <u>on your hip.</u>

Things Have Gotta Change!

Identifying and using prepositional phrases

Do your students need an extra helping of practice with prepositional phrases? Then treat them to this can't-be-beat guessing game. Choose one student to be It and stand in front of the class. Select another child to be the guesser and leave the room. Have the seated students brainstorm a list of changes It can make in his stance or appearance. Each change must be stated in a sentence that includes a prepositional phrase, such as "Hold a marker <u>between your fingers</u>" or "Put your left hand <u>on your hip.</u>" Write each suggestion on the overhead and ask students to identify the prepositional phrase. Then have It choose three changes from the list to make. Next, have the guesser return to the room. Ask her to read the sentences, then look at It to try to guess the three changes It has made. If the guesser identifies all three changes, let her choose the next It and guesser.

To Infinitives and Beyond!

Skill **Identifying and writing infinitive phrases**

For a grammar lesson that will stick, try this cool idea to teach infinitive phrases. First, review with students how to identify an infinitive phrase (see page 4). Then point out that many popular or famous sayings include infinitive phrases. Write this sentence on the board: "To teach is to touch lives forever." Have students identify the two infinitive phrases in this sentence (*to teach* and *to touch*). Challenge students to name other examples of sayings that begin with or include an infinitive phrase.

Next, give each child a sentence strip. Direct him to think of a saying that begins with one of the infinitive phrases shown. Have him write his saying on scrap paper; then have him use markers to write and illustrate the saying on the sentence strip to create a bumper sticker. After students have shared their work, post the bumper stickers on a bulletin board. If desired, staple a blank sheet of paper to the board. During the week, challenge students to list actual bumper stickers they see that include infinitive phrases. Award extra credit points to each child who contributes to the list.

(see page 4)

To read is to discover new worlds!

Phrase Craze

Skill **Identifying different types of phrases**

Make grammar practice a hands-on treat with this fun art activity. After reviewing with students four types of phrases—appositive, gerund, infinitive, prepositional—give each child a 12" x 18" sheet of construction paper, a glue stick, scissors, a marker, a highlighter, and several old magazines. Have each child fold her paper in half two times; then have her unfold her paper and trace over the fold lines to create four sections. Direct the student to label each section with a phrase type as shown. Then challenge her to search through the magazines and highlight sentences that include examples of the four phrase types. Have the student underline the phrase in each highlighted sentence; then have her cut out each sentence and glue it collage-style in the appropriate section of her poster. When students are finished, post the collages on a bulletin board titled "Phrase Craze."

Phrase Fries

Identifying different types of phrases

If you're hungry for a fun way to teach students how to identify types of phrases, here's a game that's made to order! For each group, make four copies of the french fries box on page 12 (copy the pattern on red paper or have students color their boxes with a red marker). Also make one copy of the patterns below on yellow paper for each group. Follow these simple steps to prepare and play this nifty game for small groups of three or four students.

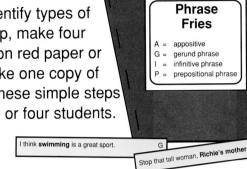

Phrase Fries

A = appositive
G = gerund phrase
I = infinitive phrase
P = prepositional phrase

I think **swimming** is a great sport.　　G

Stop that tall woman, **Richie's mother.**　　A

To prepare:
1. Cut out each fry box pattern. Fold on the center bold line. Unfold.
2. Fold on the dotted lines. Lightly crease, then unfold.
3. Fold on the center bold line again. Staple the sides to form a pocket.
4. Cut out the labels. Glue one to each fry box as shown.
5. Cut out the 20 fries below.
6. Fold back the letter on each fry. Tape the folded portion to the back of the fry to conceal the code letter.
7. Place the fries in one of the Phrase Fries boxes.

Directions for 3–4 players:
1. Choose one player to be the Fry Dude. The Fry Dude keeps the box containing the french fries and checks the other players' answers.
2. Give an empty fry box to each of the other players.
3. Player 1 draws a fry from the Fry Dude's box. He reads the sentence and identifies the type of phrase that is boldfaced.
4. The Fry Dude takes the fry from Player 1 and turns it over to check the answer. If Player 1 is correct, the Fry Dude gives him the french fry to put in his box. If Player 1 is incorrect, the Fry Dude returns the french fry to the box holding the other fries.
5. Player 2 takes her turn by repeating Steps 3–4.
6. The game is over when all of the fries have been won or time runs out. The player with the most fries in his box wins.

French Fry Patterns
Copy on yellow paper.

Raleigh, **the capital of North Carolina,** is a growing city.	A	I want **to play football very much.**	I
The school secretary, **Mrs. Roberts,** stays very busy.	A	Linda wanted **to go on the field trip.**	I
Stop that tall woman, **Richie's mother.**	A	How badly do you want **to practice?**	I
My favorite magazine, ***Sports Illustrated for Kids,*** is fun to read.	A	She seemed **to feel bad.**	I
My neighbor, **Sharon Hayes,** is a terrific cook.	A	Bill hopes **to become a doctor.**	I
I think **swimming** is a great sport.	G	There's a rock **in my pocket.**	P
Looking for my lost dog took three hours.	G	**Over the hill** is my grandma's house.	P
Her staying at my house was a neat surprise.	G	Is that your book **on the shelf?**	P
My being at the meeting was important to our group.	G	That book was written **by Beverly Cleary.**	P
Singing is one of my favorite hobbies.	G	Lisa went to the party **with Hannah.**	P

The Joys of Toys

You like toys, right? But do you know where your favorite ones came from? Each paragraph about toys below contains four sentences. Write the simple subject of each sentence in the numbered game space. Write the simple predicate below it. The first one is done for you.

A teacher in England created the first jigsaw puzzle in 1767. It was a map of England and Wales. The pieces did not lock together. Interlocking puzzles were sold more than 100 years later.

1. *teacher created* 2. 3. 4.

People tossed empty pie tins for fun in the 1870s. Walter Morrison made a metal tossing toy in the early 1950s. The disc was remade later with plastic. Morrison named the toy Frisbee® after the company that made the pie tins.

4. 3. 2. 1.

Charles Darrow created the popular game Monopoly®. Darrow asked a toy company to sell his game. The company sold many of the games during Christmas in 1934. Charles Darrow became a very rich man.

1. 2. 3. 4.

The yo-yo was a hunting weapon in the Philippines. Donald Duncan saw it when he visited the Philippines in the 1920s. Duncan experimented with the yo-yo. He sold his smaller version as a toy in the United States.

4. 3. 2. 1.

Bonus Box: On the back of this page or on another sheet of paper, write four sentences that describe your favorite toy *without* naming it. Challenge a friend to read the sentences and identify the toy.

A Swiss Cheese Sundae?

Tom is trying to trap three tricky mice by using their favorite ice-cream sundae flavors. Read each sentence. Then write the letter beside it in order on the correct sundae. The first one has been done for you. When you're finished, you'll discover each animal's favorite sundae flavor.

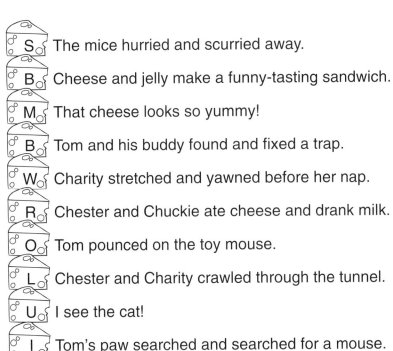

S — The mice hurried and scurried away.

B — Cheese and jelly make a funny-tasting sandwich.

M — That cheese looks so yummy!

B — Tom and his buddy found and fixed a trap.

W — Charity stretched and yawned before her nap.

R — Chester and Chuckie ate cheese and drank milk.

O — Tom pounced on the toy mouse.

L — Chester and Charity crawled through the tunnel.

U — I see the cat!

I — Tom's paw searched and searched for a mouse.

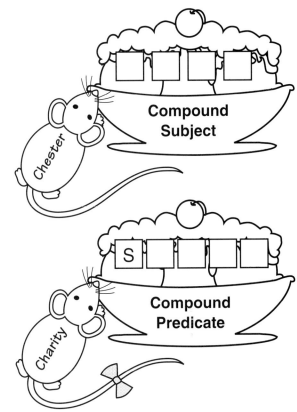

Compound Subject

Compound Predicate

Compound Subject & Predicate

None of the above

 S — Chuckie ran and hid from Tom.

 I — Chuckie and Charity nibbled and swallowed the cheese.

 U — Morning, noon, and night are fine times for a nap.

 S — Chester loves checkers.

 E — The mice and their friends chuckled and laughed at the silly cat.

 S — Charity ate and drank until she couldn't move.

 E — Chuckie's mom and dad told him to eat cheese instead of ice cream.

 E — This cheese is crumbly.

Bonus Box: On a sheet of notebook paper, write four sentences about how you spent last weekend—one for each of the four categories on the sundaes above. Skip a line after each sentence. Then challenge a friend to write the correct category under each sentence.

Patterns

Use with "Phrase Fries" on page 9.

French Fries Box

Make four copies on red paper for each group.

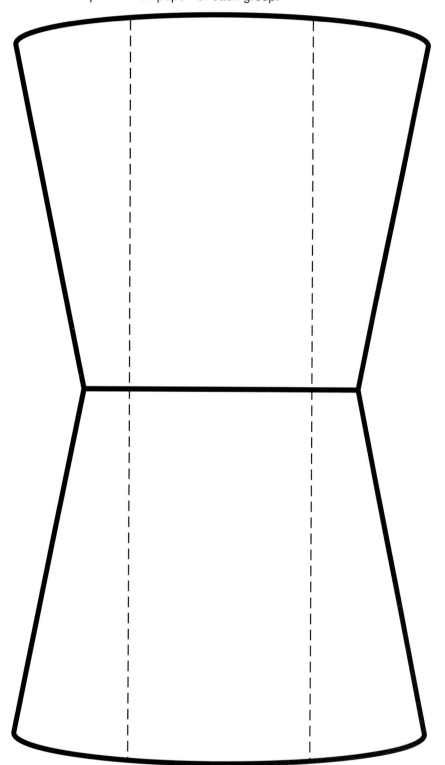

Box Labels

Phrase Fries

A = appositive
G = gerund phrase
I = infinitive phrase
P = prepositional phrase

Phrase Fries

A = appositive
G = gerund phrase
I = infinitive phrase
P = prepositional phrase

Phrase Fries

A = appositive
G = gerund phrase
I = infinitive phrase
P = prepositional phrase

Phrase Fries

A = appositive
G = gerund phrase
I = infinitive phrase
P = prepositional phrase

Googingheim's Grammar Gadget

Introducing Googingheim's amazing Grammar Gadget! This machine sorts sentences by main and subordinate clauses. But it's broken, so you'll have to do the sorting yourself. For each sentence, decide if the boldfaced part is a main clause or a subordinate clause. Then circle the correct letter. Write the circled letters in order below to read the goofy message the broken machine spit out.

> A *clause* is a group of words that has a subject and a predicate.
> A *main clause* can stand alone as a complete sentence.
>   Example: <u>Dad sold our car</u> because we needed a van.
> A *subordinate clause* gives an idea related to the main clause. It cannot stand alone as a sentence.
>   Example: Dad sold our car <u>because we needed a van</u>.

		Main	Subordinate
1.	**We blew a fuse** because the electrical outlets were too full.	F	P
2.	The sparks flew like fireworks **since the room was dark.**	K	E
3.	**Since the news leaked out,** reporters are everywhere.	B	E
4.	**Professor Googingheim will be famous** once people find out.	D	L
5.	The professor read about machines **whenever he could.**	O	M
6.	Although it took time, **the professor read over 300 books.**	E	C
7.	The machine will make millions **after the mistake is fixed.**	T	G
8.	**Googingheim painted his machine** while waiting for repairs.	R	U
9.	**Unless repairs are made soon,** the machine may never work again.	P	E
10.	**The machine must work** before school starts next week.	E	X
11.	**Until he patents the machine,** he can't tell anyone how it works.	L	N
12.	If the repair crew comes today, **the gadget will be in gear soon.**	W	K
13.	Googingheim doesn't want to be interrupted **when he is interviewed.**	Y	A
14.	So he can tell kids about the machine, **Googingheim will speak at our school.**	F	I
15.	**The professor has tried to fix the machine four times** since it broke yesterday.	F	Q
16.	**The gadget must be repaired** before it is shown to the public.	L	P
17.	**Because he'll be on television,** the professor bought a new suit.	C	E
18.	Googingheim will be a happy person **when the machine is fixed.**	R	S

INSERT

OUTPUT

Googingheim's
Grammar Gadget

MAIN CLAUSE

SUBORDINATE
CLAUSE

_ _ _ _ _ _ _
_ _ _ _ _
_ _ _ _ _ _ _ _ !

Bonus Box: Write a paragraph about a machine you'd like to invent one day. Underline each main clause. Circle each subordinate clause.

Sentence Slice

Grab a partner and play this "pizza-rrific" game that sharpens sentence skills!

Materials needed: pencil   paper clip
die   paper

Directions for two players:

1. Write your name in one of the score boxes.
2. In turn, roll the die to determine a sentence from the Sentence Box.
3. Spin to determine how to change your sentence. (See the illustration of how to use the pencil and paper clip to make a spinner.)
4. Write your new sentence on your paper. Then read it aloud to your partner.
5. If your partner agrees that the sentence is correct, make two tally marks in your score box.
6. If your partner thinks that the sentence is incorrect, ask your teacher to check it. If the sentence is correct, make two tally marks in your score box. If it is incorrect, have your partner make two tally marks in his or her score box.
7. Continue playing until time is up or one player has earned 12 points.
8. After the game, work with your partner to write six new simple sentences on a sheet of paper. If time allows, play a second game.

Sentence Box

1. Sam jumped in the mud puddle.
2. Lois rode her skateboard.
3. Tony passed the ball.
4. A bird sat on the windowsill.
5. Cara ate four cookies.
6. The dog ran away.

Player 1	Player 2

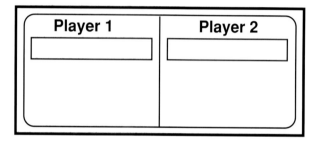

Have a slice!

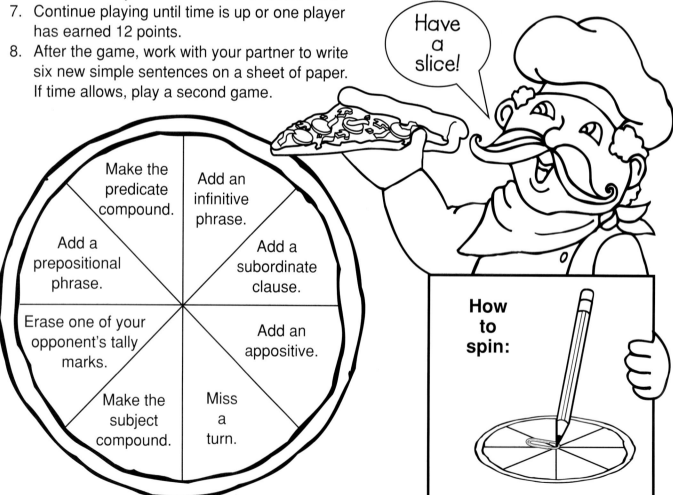

Make the predicate compound.

Add an infinitive phrase.

Add a prepositional phrase.

Add a subordinate clause.

Erase one of your opponent's tally marks.

Add an appositive.

Make the subject compound.

Miss a turn.

How to spin:

Kinds of Sentences and Their Functions

Sentences can be grouped according to what they do: make statements, ask questions, make requests, or exclaim strong feelings.

- **Declarative** sentences make statements.

  EXAMPLES   Lots of people attended today's concert.
  Caleb is a super soccer player.

- **Imperative** sentences give commands.

  EXAMPLES   Please close the door behind you.
  Place your books on that table.

- **Interrogative** sentences ask questions.

  EXAMPLES   When did you buy your tickets?
  How did Elyse make that centerpiece?

- **Exclamatory** sentences express strong emotions or feelings.

  EXAMPLES   What a scary movie that was!
  I can't believe I actually won!

A Novel Approach

Skill

Identifying kinds of sentences and their functions

Declarative = blue
Imperative = yellow
Interrogative = pink
Exclamatory = green

Use your current read-aloud book to provide students with a novel activity on identifying kinds of sentences and their functions. Make a copy of a page in the book or story your class is currently reading. Give each pair of students a copy of the page and four colored highlighters. Next, list the four kinds of sentences and their functions on the board (see page 15). After reviewing the information with students, assign a highlighter color to each kind of sentence (see the illustration). Then have each pair of students read the page and highlight the sentences according to the code on the board. Review students' answers and discuss the reasons behind their classifications.

game the a
that which play
player what terrific
won

I'm Banking on It!

Skill

Writing sentences with different functions

Give students a sporting chance at understanding the differences between the functions of sentences with this writing activity. First, write the following words on the board: *a, boy, can, did, eat, eating, ice cream, is, melting, that, the, whose.* Ask a student to use some of the words to create a declarative sentence. Write the suggested sentence on the board. Then ask the rest of the class to give examples of the other three kinds of sentences, such as:
* Whose ice cream is melting? (interrogative)
* That ice cream is melting! (exclamatory)
* Eat the ice cream. (imperative)

Point out to students that they used some of the same words to create four different kinds of sentences with four different meanings. Next, challenge each child to create a word bank of her own that contains 12 words or less. Have the student write her bank at the top of her paper; then direct her to use the words to write eight sentences (two of each kind). Allow students to revise their word banks as they work, if necessary.

After a sharing time, display the sentences on a bulletin board decorated with punctuation mark cutouts and the title "Write sentences? Write sentences!"

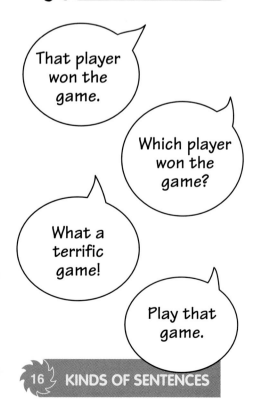

That player won the game.

Which player won the game?

What a terrific game!

Play that game.

Say What?

Identifying kinds of sentences

Listen up! That's exactly what your students will do when they complete this fun activity on identifying kinds of sentences. First, have each student make a chart as shown on a sheet of unlined paper.

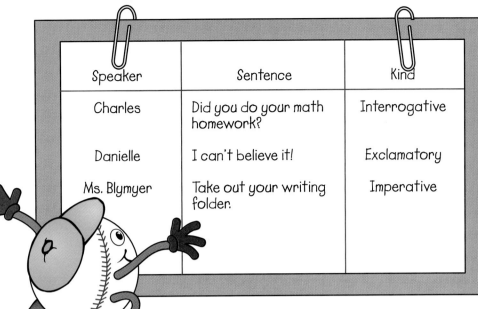

Speaker	Sentence	Kind
Charles	Did you do your math homework?	Interrogative
Danielle	I can't believe it!	Exclamatory
Ms. Blymyer	Take out your writing folder.	Imperative

Then have him use two jumbo paper clips to attach the chart to a sturdy piece of cardboard or a large panel cut from an empty cereal box. Direct the student to carry his chart with him throughout the day and record examples of each kind of sentence as he hears them in conversations or class discussions. (Remind students that eavesdropping is not allowed.) Beside each sentence, have the student write the name of the speaker as shown. At the end of the day, let students share examples of the sentences they wrote for each category.

Please throw the ball to me!

Imperative

Sentence Kickball

Creating different kinds of sentences

Mix a game of kickball with grammar and what have you got? Practice that's just plain fun! On a sunny day, head to the playground to play Sentence Kickball. First, place a strip of masking tape on each base. Then label each tape strip with a kind of sentence. Use the rules of kickball with one variation: at the end of a play, each student standing on a base must give a sentence that matches the base's label in order to stay there. If the sentence is incorrect, the student is out. If a player has just tagged home base, she must return and give a correct sentence in order to score the run. For an extra challenge, announce a category (such as animals, sports, or a topic your class is studying) at the beginning of each new inning; then require that students give only sentences related to that category.

Sentence Sort

Identifying kinds of sentences

For a grammar activity that's sure to be a hit with students, take a swing at this idea! Use the patterns below to make 20 baseball cutouts on white construction paper and 4 mitt cutouts on brown construction paper. Write each of the sentences shown on a numbered ball cutout. Label each mitt cutout with a kind of sentence. If desired, laminate the baseballs and mitts for durability. Then make an answer key to place with the cutouts in a large zippered plastic bag. During free time, challenge students to match each ball to the correct mitt and check their work with the answer key.

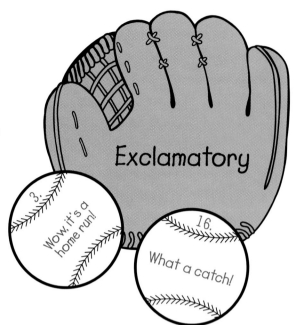

1. Is that a dog running on the field (INT)
2. Ask the coach if I can pitch today (IMP)
3. Wow, it's a home run (E)
4. We play the Rockets today at 3:00 (D)
5. Our team colors are red and blue this year (D)
6. Step up to the plate (IMP)
7. I'm so excited about the big game (E)
8. Why didn't you throw the ball to Jamie (INT)
9. Come to practice on time Wednesday (IMP)
10. The game will be on television tonight (D)
11. How many people attended that game (INT)
12. Boy, that sure wasn't an out (E)
13. That player is their best hitter (D)
14. How did you learn to pitch so well (INT)
15. My baseball shoes are too small for me (D)
16. What a catch (E)
17. Are you going to miss practice today (INT)
18. Show good sportsmanship today (IMP)
19. Make sure your uniform is ready (IMP)
20. That guy can run (E)

Patterns

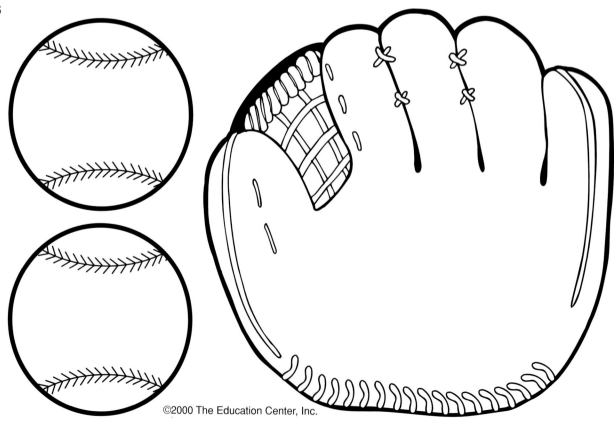

18

Grammar Golf, Anyone?

Time to tee up at the Great Grammar Golf Course! It's a challenging course. To complete it successfully, use the code to color the flag at each hole according to the kind of sentence written beside it. When you're finished, add a punctuation mark after each sentence.

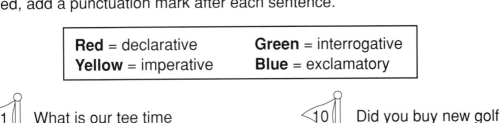

Red = declarative	**Green** = interrogative
Yellow = imperative	**Blue** = exclamatory

1 What is our tee time

2 This course opened three years ago

3 Drive the golf cart for the first nine holes

4 Can I borrow your putter

5 We will have lunch in the clubhouse

6 That runaway golf cart is heading straight for us

7 Give me your money so I can pay the greens fee

8 I just beat the course record

9 The groundskeeper does an excellent job taking care of the course

10 Did you buy new golf shoes

11 We should be finished with the course before lunch

12 Have you ever hit a ball in a lake or sand trap

13 We will need to return to the clubhouse if it starts to storm

14 Take your shot so we can move to the next hole

15 Wow, that was a super shot

16 Do you want to go golfing again next Saturday

17 Meet me here at 8:00

18 I shot a hole in one

Bonus Box: On the back of this page or on another sheet of paper, write four sentences about your favorite sport—one for each kind of sentence listed above.

The Great Sentence Search

Ready to go on a search for the four kinds of sentences? Fill in the chart with sentences that you might hear at each of the events listed. Two examples are given.

A *declarative sentence* makes a statement.
An *imperative sentence* gives a command.
An *interrogative sentence* asks a question.
An *exclamatory sentence* expresses a strong feeling or emotion.

Sentences you might hear…	Imperative	Exclamatory	Interrogative	Declarative
at your birthday party				
on the first day of school			Whose class are you in?	
at a football game		We won the game!		
in the cafeteria lunch line				
after you receive an A on a big test				

Bonus Box: Think of another event that you could add to the chart above. Write the event at the top of a sheet of paper or the back of this page. Then list four sentences—one for each kind—that you might hear at that event.

©2000 The Education Center, Inc. • *Grammar Plus!* • *Sentence Structure & Usage* • TEC2314

Sentence Structures

English has three basic sentence structures: simple, compound, and complex.

- A **simple sentence** has one complete subject and one complete predicate. If the subject or predicate is compound, the sentence is still simple. A simple sentence can be short or long.

EXAMPLES   The dog barked.
The spotted dog in our neighbor's yard chased the cat along the fence and into the backyard.
Ben and Bonnie cooked the meal and cleaned the dishes.

- A **compound sentence** consists of two or more simple sentences (main or independent clauses) joined by a conjunction and a comma.

EXAMPLES   Mom picked me up from school, and Dad took me to the doctor.
Rick lost my lucky penny, but I didn't stay mad at him for long.

— Sometimes a semicolon is used to join two simple sentences.

EXAMPLE   Our school had a book fair; hundreds of people came.

- A **complex sentence** consists of a main (independent) clause and a subordinate (dependent) clause that are joined by a subordinating conjunction.

EXAMPLES   Whenever I watch that movie, I always cry.
Edie won't go to the mall unless Marcie goes with her.

It doesn't matter whether the independent clause or the dependent clause comes first in the sentence.

Subordinating conjunctions include:

after	in case	unless
although	once	until
as	since	when
as if	so	whenever
because	so that	where
before	than	whereas
even though	that	wherever
for	though	whether
if	till	while

What's Your Structure?

Identifying sentence structure

Show students that they read sentences with different structures every day with this activity. Ask one-third of your students to take out their social studies textbooks. Direct another third to take out the novels they are reading. Finally, give a newspaper section to each student in the last third of the class. Instruct each child to label a sheet of paper as shown. Then have him examine 30 consecutive sentences in his reading material and mark a tally on his paper for each one as shown.

When students have finished, divide the class into three groups according to the type of reading material used. Give each group a sheet of chart paper and markers. For each group, assign a recorder to gather the data from his teammates and find the total for each sentence structure; then direct the recorder's teammates to check his computations. Finally, have each group create a graph showing the data from its surveys. Below the graph, have the group write a brief definition of each sentence structure. Display the graphs on a bulletin board titled "What's Your Structure?"

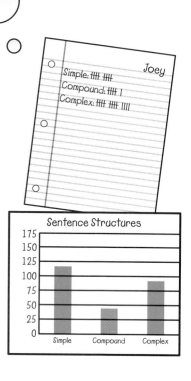

Sentence	Structure	Points
1.		
2.		
3.		
4.		
5.		
6.		
7.		
8.		
9.		
10.		

Deep-Sea Sentences

Writing and identifying sentences with different structures

Dive into a "fin-tastic" review of sentence structures with this fun challenge. Give each student a copy of page 25, a sheet of unlined paper, and a ruler. After the student fills in page 25's web, have her follow the directions in Step 2 to make the chart shown on her unlined paper. Then have her complete Steps 3–4.

Next, direct each child to swap papers and check to see if her partner correctly identified the structure of each sentence he wrote. (See Step 5 on page 25.) After students return papers to their owners, have each student complete Steps 6–7 to find her total score. Award a baggie of Goldfish® crackers to each of your top three scorers.

Sentence Builders

Writing and identifying sentences with different structures

Help students build their sentence skills with this nifty small-group game. First, have each group of three students cut 72 slips of paper. Give the group a copy of the word box below and a paper lunch bag. Then have students write one word on each slip and place the slips in the bag. When the bags are ready, give each group a die and go over the game rules that follow.

Game Rules: Player 1 rolls the die, draws that number of cards from the bag, and tries to form a sentence. If he can't he keeps his cards, then Player 2 takes a turn. Play continues in this manner until a player can form a sentence with his cards (not all cards have to be used). The player shares the sentence and announces the sentence structure. If the group members agree that the sentence is complete and generally makes sense, and that the structure given is correct, the player records the following score on his paper:

- Simple sentence = 1 point
- Compound sentence = 5 points
- Complex sentence = 8 points

If any part of the answer is incorrect or the sentence is incomplete, the player earns no points. After the score is recorded, the player returns the cards to the bag and tries to make a new sentence on his next turns. Play continues until time runs out or a player scores 12 or more points.

her | hat | is | at | the | store | so | she | will | get | it

This is a compound sentence. That's worth five points!

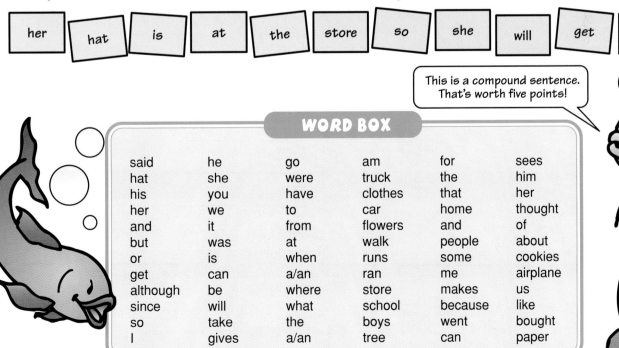

WORD BOX

said	he	go	am	for	sees
hat	she	were	truck	the	him
his	you	have	clothes	that	her
her	we	to	car	home	thought
and	it	from	flowers	and	of
but	was	at	walk	people	about
or	is	when	runs	some	cookies
get	can	a/an	ran	me	airplane
although	be	where	store	makes	us
since	will	what	school	because	like
so	take	the	boys	went	bought
I	gives	a/an	tree	can	paper

Roll With It!

 Writing compound and complex sentences

Hook students on writing compound and complex sentences correctly with this game that's a "reel" treat to play!

To get ready:

1. Pull cards 5 and up from a deck of playing cards. (Do not pull any aces.)
2. Have each student cut two or three interesting pictures from old magazines. Place all pictures in a manila envelope.
3. Cover the sides of a die (except for the 1) with small pieces of white self-sticking labels. Program each of the five covered sides with one of these punctuation marks: comma, exclamation point, question mark, apostrophe, quotation marks. Let the dot for 1 represent a period.
4. Cover the sides of a second die as in Step 3, including the 1 side. Program the sides with these words: *and, but, or, so, however, because.*

To play:

1. Divide the class into teams of four or five students each.
2. Display one magazine picture and one card from the deck.
3. Roll the dice. Write the punctuation mark and conjunction rolled on a corner of the board.
4. At your signal, each team must write a sentence (on a sheet of paper or the board) about the magazine picture. The sentence must consist of the number of words indicated by the card (a jack = 11, a queen = 12, and a king = 13). It must also include the punctuation mark and conjunction rolled.
5. At the end of three minutes, have each group read aloud its sentence and tell whether it is simple, compound, or complex. Award points according to this scale:
   - 1 point for using the correct number of words to make a complete sentence
   - 1 point for including the conjunction rolled
   - 1 point for correctly using the punctuation mark rolled
   - 2 points for correctly identifying the type of sentence written
   - 1–5 points for writing a creative sentence related to the picture (base score on creativity)
6. Repeat Steps 2–5 to play another round. At the end of the game, total the points and declare the team with the highest score the winner.

The runner crossed the finish line, and the crowd cheered for her.

Deep-Sea Sentences

Dive into this "fin-tastic" sentence-making challenge!

1. Use a pencil to write a word in each bubble below. Include nouns, verbs, adjectives, adverbs, prepositions, pronouns, and conjunctions.
2. Make a chart on your paper like the one shown.
3. On each line, write a sentence that uses words connected to each other in the web. No jumping over words! You may add words that aren't on the web, but you'll lose a point for each one (except for *a, the,* and *an*). Also, you may use words in more than one sentence.
4. Write *S* in the chart if your sentence is **simple,** *C* if it is **compound,** and *X* if it is **complex.**
5. Swap papers with a classmate. Have your partner check to see that you correctly identified the structure of each sentence. If the structure is correct, have your partner circle the sentence's code letter in the chart.
6. Swap papers back with your partner. Beside each circled code letter on your paper, write the number of points you earned for that sentence.
7. Add the points to find your total score.

	Sentence	Structure	Points
1.			
2.			
3.			
4.			
5.			
6.			
7.			
8.			
9.			
10.			

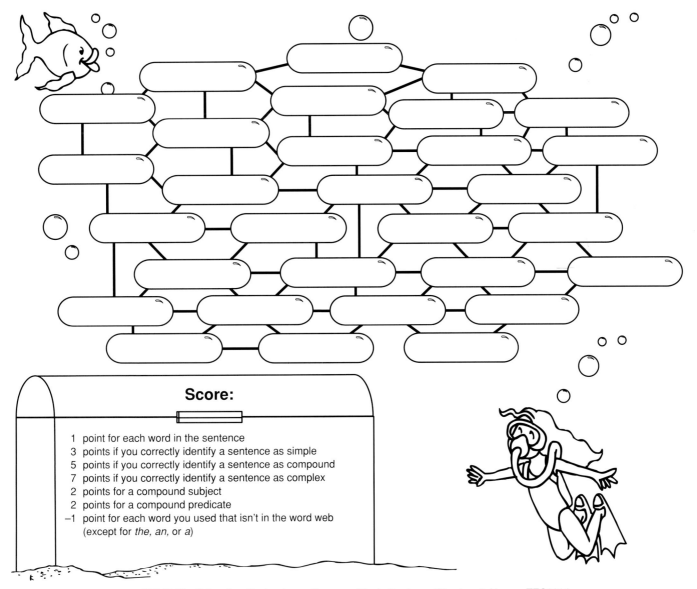

Score:

1 point for each word in the sentence
3 points if you correctly identify a sentence as simple
5 points if you correctly identify a sentence as compound
7 points if you correctly identify a sentence as complex
2 points for a compound subject
2 points for a compound predicate
−1 point for each word you used that isn't in the word web (except for *the, an,* or *a*)

©2000 The Education Center, Inc. • *Grammar Plus!* • *Sentence Structure & Usage* • TEC2314

Note to the teacher: Use with "Deep-Sea Sentences" on page 22. Provide each child with a sheet of unlined paper and a ruler.

25

What a Watercolor!

Read each sentence. In the blank beside it, write *S* if the sentence is **simple**, *C* if it is **compound**, and *X* if it is **complex**. When you're finished, color the numbered spaces below according to the code.

_____ 1. Mom packed a picnic, and we drove to the park.

_____ 2. While I'm at camp, my little brother can use my bicycle.

_____ 3. Lucky and Tiger chased each other in the backyard.

_____ 4. Before he can paint the bedroom, Bill must take down the old wallpaper.

_____ 5. I can't start my report until Mom can take me to the library.

_____ 6. Ricky sang loudly.

_____ 7. We can play cards this afternoon, or Dad can take us to the movies.

_____ 8. Alice's aunt from Detroit wrote a letter to her niece in Orlando.

_____ 9. Lulu can't go to the party because she has a cold.

_____ 10. I didn't have a temperature today, but Mom still kept me home from school.

_____ 11. Macey packed tissues in her purse since she always cries at movies.

_____ 12. That thunderstorm was incredibly dangerous; lightning struck our barn!

_____ 13. Since Mary has the lead in the play, she will need to memorize lots of lines.

_____ 14. Benny laughed and joked with his best friend.

_____ 15. My teacher asked me a question, and I gave the correct answer.

_____ 16. Unless it stops raining soon, the game will be canceled.

S =	blue
C =	red
X =	yellow

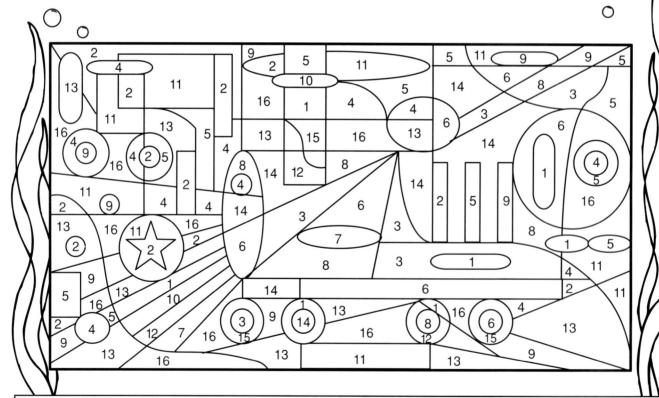

Bonus Box: What famous person in the present or the past would you just LOVE to spend one hour with? On the back of this page or another sheet or paper, write three sentences about the time you would spend with this hero: one simple, one compound, and one complex. Then give the sentences to a classmate. Challenge him or her to identify each sentence's structure.

Sentence Errors

Writers sometimes make errors when they write sentences. Three common mistakes are sentence fragments, run-on sentences, and rambling sentences.

- A **sentence fragment** is a group of words that is missing the subject, main verb, or both. A sentence fragment does not express a complete thought.

EXAMPLES   Flapped loudly. *(missing the subject)*
The curtains on my bedroom window. *(missing the verb)*
Because of the wind. *(missing the subject and the verb)*

How to fix a sentence fragment: Add the information that is missing so that the sentence expresses a complete thought.

EXAMPLE   The curtains on my bedroom window.

FIXED   The curtains on my bedroom window flapped loudly in the breeze.

Another way to fix a sentence fragment is to remove a word that keeps the sentence from being complete:

EXAMPLE   Rachel, who has been my best friend for years.

FIXED   Rachel has been my best friend for years.

• A **run-on sentence** is two or more sentences joined together without the correct punctuation or conjunction.

EXAMPLE We were so busy today the yard had to be mowed flowers had to be planted we worked for hours.

How to fix a run-on sentence: Add the proper punctuation or a connecting word. Also add capital letters where needed.

EXAMPLES We were so busy today. The yard had to be mowed. Flowers had to be planted. We worked for hours.

We were so busy today. The yard had to be mowed and flowers had to be planted. We worked for hours.

• A **rambling sentence** is one in which too many little sentences are strung together with the conjunction *and.*

EXAMPLE Our class went to the zoo and we toured the exhibits and everyone ate a picnic lunch and the ride home was really cool.

How to fix a rambling sentence: Delete some of the *and*s. Add proper capital letters and punctuation.

EXAMPLE Our class went to the zoo. We toured the exhibits and everyone ate a picnic lunch. The ride home was really cool.

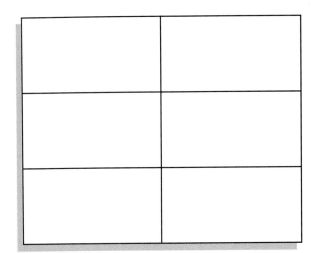

Then he saw Beezus and Ramona coming Beezus's real name was Beatrice.

R

DG

Identifying sentence errors

Help students learn to recognize sentence errors in a snap with this literature-linked activity. Have each child cut a sheet of unlined paper into six sections as shown. On each section, have the child write a sentence from the novel he's currently reading, changing each into a fragment, run-on, or rambling sentence. Direct the child to label the back of each slip with his initials and a letter(s) to indicate the error: F = fragment, R = run-on, RA = rambling. Then collect the sentences.

Next, divide the class into groups. Give each group a handful of sentence slips. Then instruct the students to sort their sentences into three piles according to the errors. Have the group check the back of each slip to make sure it is placed in the correct pile. Encourage students to confer with a sentence's writer if they disagree with the error it represents. Finally, collect the slips again and give a new set to each group. At the end of the activity, collect the slips; then give a few to each student to correct on his own paper.

The Parent Trap

Identifying and correcting sentence errors

Get parents into the act with this kid-pleasin' activity. Have each child take home three sentence strips with instructions for a parent to label each one with an example of a sentence error. (Send home copies of pages 27 and 28 too, as parents will probably need a bit of review.) Ask parents to write their child's name at the bottom of each completed strip as shown. The next day collect the strips; then post three of them on a small bulletin board titled "The Parent Trap!" Tell students that their parents are going to try to trap them with their tricky sentences; then challenge each child to escape the parent trap by correcting the sentences in his journal by the end of the day. Before dismissal, discuss the errors and how to correct them. Then tally how many students escaped the trap by rewriting the sentences correctly. Post three different sentences for the next day. Continue until all sentences have been shared with the class.

Watch Out for
The Parent Trap!

Philip went shopping and he bought a video game and he ate at the food court.
Philip

Meg, who is a great ballerina.
Meg

Ryan studied for his test for an hour he made an A!
Ryan

Find and Fix 'Em!

Identifying and correcting sentence errors

Run-Ons

- The princess curtsied and asked the prince about the castle he looked puzzled.

- When the ball hit, I was so surprised I ducked the pitcher dove for it.

- I have never liked broccoli cauliflower isn't a favorite of mine either.

Where's the best place for students to find and fix sentence errors? Their own writing, of course! Post three sheets of chart paper labeled "Fragments," "Run-Ons," and "Rambling" at the front of the classroom. After reviewing these errors, have each child pull out a writing sample, such as a story or a journal entry. Divide the class into groups and have each group sit in a circle. Direct each student to pass her writing to the classmate on her left. Then give students three or four minutes to read the writings and look for fragments, run-ons, and rambling sentences. If a student finds an error, she goes to the front of the room and uses a marker to write the sentence on the correct chart. Continue having students pass papers until each chart has been labeled with two or three sentences. Then have the class decide together whether each sentence is written on the appropriate chart and how the error could be corrected. Remind students not to mention who made the mistakes but to focus on how the mistakes can be fixed. Repeat this activity throughout the year to keep those "find-it-and-fix-it" skills well-oiled!

Today's Topic

Identifying and correcting sentence errors

Turn students into mistake-free sentence mechanics with this nifty activity! Write the topics below on slips of paper; then place the slips in a container. Ask a student to pull a slip from the container and announce the topic. Then divide the class into pairs. Have each pair write a sentence related to the topic that is either a fragment, a run-on, or a rambling sentence. When students are finished, have one pair at a time display its sentence (on the board or overhead) and challenge classmates to identify and correct the error. Repeat the activity whenever you want to practice other grammar or writing skills.

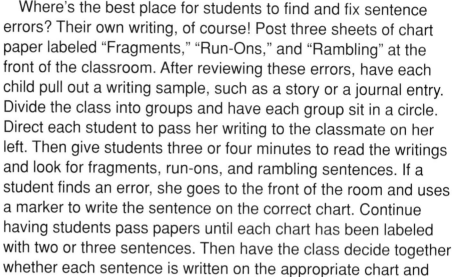

TOPICS

extreme sports	fame
music videos	heroes
homework	television shows
parents	eating out
little brothers and sisters	tests
bad habits	the perfect school
life in the future	computers
dream vacations	

It's a Bird...It's a Plane...It's Grammar Man!

Skill **Identifying and correcting sentence errors**

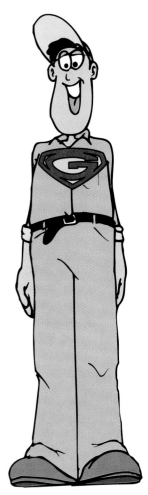

Who you gonna call when sentences need some serious error repair? Find out when you play this fun team game! Enlarge, color, and cut out the pattern below. Laminate the pattern if desired. Also label 20 tagboard strips with sentences that include sentence errors. (Check your grammar textbook for examples.)

To play, divide the class into four teams. Post a sentence strip on the board. Then give each team one minute to discuss the type of error represented and how to correct it. When time is up, have a player from Team 1 come to the board, identify the error, and explain how to correct it. If his answer is correct, tape the Grammar Man sign on his shirt; then give his team one point. If the answer is incorrect, ask a player from Team 2 to explain her team's answer. The next player to correctly identify and fix a sentence's error "captures" the Grammar Man emblem to wear on his shirt. Play until all sentences have been used. Award three bonus points to the team that possesses the Grammar Man emblem at the game's end. Then total the final score for each team and declare the winner.

Use with the idea above. **Pattern**

Name —————————————————

Correcting sentence errors

Positively Puzzled!

Each numbered box below contains a puzzle. Unfortunately, each puzzle includes several errors, such as sentence fragments, run-on sentences, and rambling sentences. Rewrite each puzzle on your paper to correct the errors.

1.
The camp cook. Wanted to measure four ounces of syrup. Out of a jug. He had only a five-ounce and a three-ounce pitcher how did he do it?

2.
A sudden thunderstorm overturned a canoe and a girl swam to a rocky island and she rested in a deserted hut. She found an old kerosene lamp. And a few matches. The wood on the island was too wet to build a fire the lamp was her only way to signal for help. But the lamp held only an inch of kerosene and that wasn't enough to reach the lamp's short wick how did she get the lamp to burn so she could signal for help?

3.
The electricity was off in a boy's bedroom and he needed to find a clean pair of socks and his socks were all exactly alike. Except that half were black and half were brown. How many socks does he have to pull out. Before he is sure of getting a matched pair?

4.

A square house has four walls and each wall has a window and each window faces the south. A bear. Walks by the window what color is the bear?

5.
A deep-sea fishing boat is docked in a harbor a rope ladder hangs over the boat's side. The end of the ladder. Is just touching the water. The rungs of the ladder are one foot apart and the tide is rising eight inches an hour how many rungs will be covered by water in two hours?

When you're finished:

Now, can you figure out the solutions to these puzzling problems? Find a partner and discuss each puzzle. Write your answers on the back of your own paper. Pleasant puzzling!

Bonus Box: Do you like a good puzzle? Or do you think puzzles are usually boring? On your paper, write your answer in a letter to the editor of *Puzzle Power* magazine.

©2000 The Education Center, Inc. • *Grammar Plus! • Sentence Structure & Usage* • TEC2314 • Key pp. 47 & 48

Subject-Verb Agreement in Sentences

One tricky element of good writing is subject-verb agreement. The subject and verb in a sentence must agree, or be the same, in person and number.

- In a sentence, the subject and verb must agree in **person** (first, second, or third).
  — Use a first-person verb with a first-person subject.

  EXAMPLE   I talk on the phone a lot.

  —Use a second-person verb with a second-person subject.

  EXAMPLE   You talk on the phone a lot.

  —Use a third-person verb with a third-person subject.

  EXAMPLE   He talks on the phone a lot.

- The subject and verb must also agree in **number** (singular or plural).
  — Use a singular verb with a singular subject.

  EXAMPLE   The whale leaps.

  —Use a plural verb with a plural subject.

  EXAMPLE   The whales leap.

- A **collective noun** names a group of things, people, or animals. Usually a collective noun is used with a singular verb because a group usually acts together as a single unit.

  EXAMPLES   The group of teachers is in the library.
  That herd of elephants was huge!

- **Compound subjects joined by** *and* are plural and need plural verbs.

  EXAMPLE   The **boys and girls** learn how to square-dance at our school.

- Sometimes **two food words** are used together so frequently that they are considered **one dish.** Use a singular verb with these subjects.

  EXAMPLE   **Spaghetti and meatballs** is my favorite meal.

- When a **compound subject** is **joined by or,** use a verb that matches the subject closer to the verb. To find out whether the subject and verb in this kind of sentence agree, read only the subject closer to the verb and the verb. It they agree, then the compound subject agrees with the verb.

  EXAMPLES   **Bill or I** lead the class each Monday.
  Mrs. Smith or Mr. Haney cooks the dinner.

- **Indefinite pronouns** are words that refer to nouns in a nonspecific way. Some are singular, some are plural, and some can be either.

  EXAMPLES   **Singular:** another, anybody, anyone, anything, each, either, everybody, everyone, everything, much, neither, nobody, no one, nothing, one, somebody, someone, something

  Plural: both, few, many, others, several

  Singular or plural: all, any, most, none, some

  — If the noun (or pronoun) that the indefinite pronoun refers to is something that cannot be counted one by one, the indefinite pronoun is singular and needs a singular verb.

  EXAMPLE   **None** of his **homework was** finished by 9:00.

  —If the indefinite pronoun refers to a noun (or pronoun) that can be counted one by one, it is plural and needs a plural verb.

  EXAMPLE   **None** of his **friends were** at the game.

If You Play Your Cards Right...

Subject-verb agreement

Put subject-verb agreement skills to the test with this game. Have each child label eight index cards with two singular nouns, two singular verbs, two plural nouns, and two plural verbs (one word per card). Divide the class into groups of three to five. Then direct students in each group to combine their cards to make one deck.

To play, each player draws a card. The student holding the card that comes first alphabetically is the dealer and goes first. Students return the cards to the deck. The dealer deals four cards to each player. Each player looks at his cards to see if he can match a subject card with a verb card so that the two agree. If so, he lays the cards down. To begin his turn, the dealer then draws a card. If he can match a subject with a verb, he lays the pair on the table. If not, he keeps the card and the next player takes her turn. If a player has more than four cards in his hand, he must place one card in the discard pile. Play continues until a player makes four correct pairs.

bear

growls

We're a perfect match!

The raccoons and I

are playing.

A Perfect Match

Subject-verb agreement

All you need for this super agreement activity is a sentence strip for every pair of students. Use a black marker to label each strip with a subject and verb (singular or plural) that agree, such as "Linda runs." Cut each strip to separate the subject and verb. Then place the pieces in a bag. Have each student draw a strip from the bag. Then give the signal for each child to find a classmate with a strip that agrees and makes sense with his. After two students find each other, have them write a sentence using their subject and verb. Provide time for sharing. Then have each pair flip their strips and use a red crayon or marker to label them with a new subject and verb. Collect the strips and repeat the activity using the red words only.

Stay With the Group!

Agreement with collective nouns

Think art and grammar don't really mix? You'll think differently after this activity on collective nouns! Display the list of collective nouns shown. Remind students that a collective noun usually needs a singular verb since a group usually acts as a single unit. Next, direct each student to divide a 12" x 18" sheet of white construction paper into six sections. At the top of each section, have the student write an alliterative sentence using one of the collective nouns on the board, a prepositional phrase that describes the noun, and a verb. For example, "An army of angry ants is approaching." Then have the student illustrate the sentence. Display this collection of collective noun masterpieces on a bulletin board titled "The Scoop on Groups."

COLLECTIVE NOUNS

army, audience, band, batch, bouquet, bunch, cast, class, club, colony, committee, crew, crowd, duo, family, fleet, flock, gang, group, herd, jury, pack, school, stack, staff, swarm, team, tribe, trio, troop

Body Language

Agreement with indefinite pronouns

Undecided about indefinite pronouns? They can be confusing since they can be singular, plural, or either! Help your students combat the confusion with this movement activity. After reviewing indefinite pronouns, have students stand at their desks. Announce an indefinite pronoun (see the list on page 34). If the pronoun is singular, each student makes an *S* with his body as shown. If the pronoun is plural, a student puts his left hand on his waist to form a *P*. If the pronoun can be either singular or plural, the student makes an *E* shape by sticking both arms and his left leg out to the left. Follow up this active practice by having students complete the reproducible activity on page 40.

Compound Contest

Agreement with compound subjects joined by *and* or *or*

Help students come to an agreement about using verbs with compound subjects by playing this fun game! Copy and cut apart the game cards on page 38. Place the cards in a container. Draw on the board a simple game trail of 16–20 spaces (see the illustration). For each team, attach a different-colored paper circle to START with a small piece of tape. Finally, divide the class into three or four teams and play the game according to the following rules.

To play:

1. A student from Team 1 draws a card and reads it aloud.
2. The team decides if the verb used should be singular or plural.
3. If the answer is correct, one team member moves the team's marker forward on the game trail: one space if the verb is singular, two spaces if the verb is plural. If the team's answer is incorrect, its marker is not moved and the next team takes a turn.
4. If the team can correctly name a verb to use with the compound subject on the card, move the team's marker forward an extra space.
5. The first team to reach FINISH is the winner.

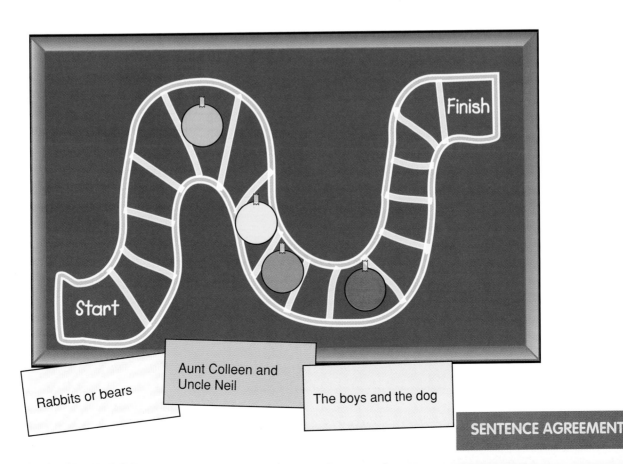

Game Cards

Use with "Compound Contest" on page 37.

The trees and bushes	The girls and Buford	Rabbits or bears
Bobby and Josiah	Buford and the girls	Mrs. Cates or Mr. Hensley
A hippo and a giraffe	A snake and two lizards	My friends or I
Poison oak and poison ivy	The students and Mrs. Miller	Ants or a ladybug
My friends and I	Parents and teachers	The girls or Buford
The butterflies and moths	Amy, Jo, and Beth	The ranger or the hunter
Aunt Colleen and Uncle Neil	Lions, tigers, and bears	The clouds or the sun
A fish and three tadpoles	Cars, trucks, and planes	Paper or pencils
The pet store and the dry cleaner	The boys and the dog	Tiger or Spot
A robin and some wrens	A hawk and an eagle	Amy, Jo, or Beth

Goin' on a Bear Hunt!

Buford and Troop 37 are on a hunt to photograph bears. Read each sentence and circle the letter of the correct verb. Then use your pencil to shade in the grid squares according to the directions for each letter. If you choose the correct words, you'll find the bears!

1. Buford and his pals _____ on a bear hunt each year.
   a. goes *(up 3)*   b. go *(up 4)*

2. Buford _____ to see bears in the wild.
   a. wants *(right 5)*   b. want *(right 2)*

3. Bob or Beulah _____ a camera.
   a. is taking *(down 1)*   b. are taking *(down 3)*

4. Either Buford or the others _____ extra food.
   a. takes *(right 4)*   b. take *(right 5)*

5. Bernice _____ the first-aid kit.
   a. brings *(up 7)*   b. bring *(down 1)*

6. The gang of Bear Cubs _____ ready to go.
   a. is *(left 3)*   b. are *(right 3)*

7. Each of them _____ around for signs of bears.
   a. looks *(down 2)*   b. look *(up 2)*

8. A trail of paw prints _____ along the stream.
   a. runs *(left 5)*   b. run *(left 3)*

9. The group _____ cautiously along the trail.
   a. tiptoe *(up 5)*   b. tiptoes *(up 10)*

10. Suddenly sounds _____ their ears.
    a. reaches *(right 4)*   b. reach *(right 6)*

11. Bob and Beulah _____ behind a bush.
    a. jumps *(up 4)*   b. jump *(down 4)*

12. A slew of bears _____ through the trees.
    a. crashes *(right 8)*   b. crash *(left 2)*

13. Either Bob or Beulah quickly _____ a photo.
    a. snaps *(down 3)*   b. snap *(up 2)*

14. Buford and the others _____ everything and run!
    a. drops *(right 3)*   b. drop *(left 2)*

15. The pictures _____ to the troop's scrapbook.
    a. is added *(up 4)*   b. are added *(down 6)*

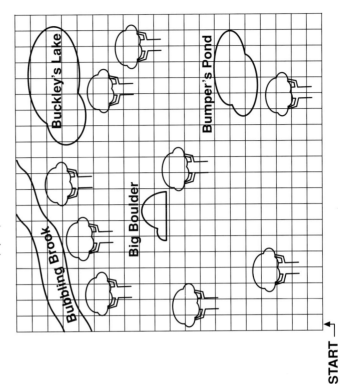

START →

©2000 The Education Center, Inc. • *Grammar Plus!* • *Sentence Structure & Usage* • TEC2314 • Key p. 48

Bonus Box: Pretend you are part of Buford's troop. Write a paragraph of at least five sentences about the bear hunt. Make sure the subject and verb agree in each sentence.

Name_____

Agreement with indefinite pronouns

In Bigfoot's Footsteps

Are you ready to track down Bigfoot, mysterious creature of the deep woods? Each sentence below contains an indefinite pronoun. Circle the indefinite pronoun; then color the footprint with the correct verb.

1. Nobody _____ been able to catch sight of this creature. (has) (have)

2. Several _____ claimed to have spotted it by Big Boulder. (has) (have)

3. Some of these people _____ planning an expedition to track it down. (is) (are)

4. Everyone _____ hoping they will find it. (is) (are)

(is) (are) 5. "Nothing _____ going to stop us from achieving our goal!" says one of the hunters.

(is) (are) 6. "Everything _____ ready for the expedition!" reports another.

(doubts) (doubt) 7. Few of the group members _____ that they will succeed.

(is) (are) 8. "Anyone _____ welcome to join us," invites the leader.

9. No one _____ the group, however. (joins) (join)

10. All of the area _____ to be covered in this expedition. (is) (are)

11. Suddenly everyone _____ eerie cries from the hills! (hears) (hear)

12. Several in the crowd _____ to the hunters to see what they'll do. (look) (looks)

(gazes) (gaze) 13. Each of the hunters _____ at the others.

(say) (says) 14. Someone _____, "Raise your hand if you have changed your mind about going."

(puts) (put) 15. Everyone _____ his hand into the air!

Bonus Box: What other mysterious creature have you heard or read about? Write a paragraph about it. Use at least five indefinite pronouns.

40   ©2000 The Education Center, Inc. • *Grammar Plus!* • *Sentence Structure & Usage* • TEC2314 • Key p. 48

# Usage

 The English language can sometimes be tricky, particularly in the use of some words and phrases. Intermediate students frequently make writing errors when using the following:

- **Homonyms** are words that are pronounced or written alike but have different meanings. Homonyms include homophones and homographs.

  EXAMPLES   *bear* and *bare*
  bay (a kind of window) and *bay* (a body of water)
  object (something material) and *object* (to oppose something)

- **Homophones** are words that sound alike but have different meanings and sometimes different spellings. Homophones can also refer to two or more different graphemes that represent the same sound, such as *kn* and *n, f* and *ph,* etc.

  EXAMPLES   *bear* and *bare*
  scale (as on a fish) and *scale* (to climb)

- **Homographs** are words that are spelled alike but have different meanings and may be pronounced differently.

  EXAMPLES   *fly* (insect) and *fly* (to become airborne)
  object (something material) and *object* (to oppose something)

- A **double negative** is the presence of more than one negative word in a sentence to convey a negative meaning. To correct a double negative, change a negative word into a positive one.

  EXAMPLE   He can't tell nobody that story. ➜ He can't tell anybody that story.

  — If the double negative contains *barely, hardly,* or *scarcely,* change the other negative word into a positive one.

  EXAMPLE   She had barely nothing left. ➜ She had barely anything left.

- **Easily confused** and **misused words** are words that sound alike or look alike.

  EXAMPLES   *accept* and *except*
  breath and *breathe*

What's the Story?

 Skill **Using homophones**

hour
our

scene
seen

Here's an activity on homophones that's sure to win everyone's stamp of approval! Write each homophone pair below on an index card. Place a card on each student's desk. Also write the following story starter on the board: "I knew it was going to be a weird day when…" Then have each student copy the starter on his paper and begin writing a story that includes the homophones on his card. Direct the student to underline each homophone on his paper after using it. After five minutes, ring a bell or signal with another noisemaker; then have each child move to the desk behind him and continue his story, incorporating the new pair of homophones into it. Continue until students have changed seats at least five times. Then announce that the next seat change will be the last one and that students should wrap up their stories. After this last rotation, have students return to their seats, read over their stories, and decide whether they have used each homophone correctly. (Have students complete this final step in pairs, if desired.) Let volunteers share their homophone tales with the class.

HOMOPHONE PAIRS

ate–eight	hour–our	right–write
bear–bare	knot–not	role–roll
blew–blue	loan–lone	scene–seen
buy–by	made–maid	sea–see
close–clothes	mail–male	some–sum
dear–deer	miner–minor	sore–soar
flew–flu	one–won	sweet–suite
hare–hair	pain–pane	their–there
hear–here	passed–past	through–threw
heel–heal	principal–principle	waist–waste

Just Say No (But Only Once!)

 Skill **Recognizing and correcting double negatives**

Stop the delivery of double negatives with this letter-perfect activity! Collect a different everyday object for each student, such as a coin, a paper clip, etc. Have students brainstorm a list of negative words (such as the ones shown) as you list them on the board. Also go over how to correct double negatives (see page 41). Next, give one object, a small overhead transparency, and an overhead pen to each student. On her transparency, have the student write a sentence with a double negative about her object (see the example). Collect the objects and place them on a table. Then have one student come to the table and remove an object other than her own. The child who wrote about that object comes to the overhead, displays her sentence, and calls on a volunteer to correct it. If correct, the volunteer chooses the next classmate to remove an object from the table. If incorrect, the writer calls on another classmate. Continue until every child has shared her sentence.

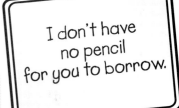
I don't have no pencil for you to borrow.

Negative words: *no, nobody, nothing, nowhere, none, never, no one, nor, neither, not, hardly, scarcely, barely.* Also includes any contraction made with *not,* such as *didn't, mustn't, weren't,* etc.

We've Got Homographs in the Bag!

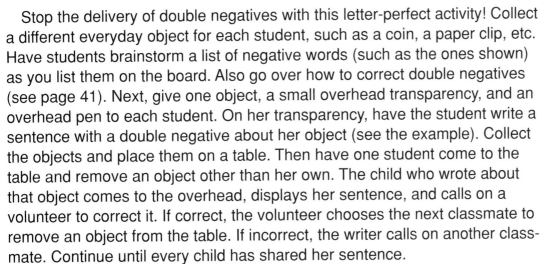

 Skill **Using homographs**

Bag better usage skills with this nifty activity! Write the words shown below on chart paper. Assign one word to each student. Direct the student to find her word in a dictionary and list its different meanings (and, if applicable, pronunciations). Then give each child a small paper bag with instructions to fill it with objects and/or pictures that illustrate her word's different meanings. For example, a student assigned *ruler* might bring a measuring device and a picture of a world leader. Allow several days for students to fill their bags.

After all objects have been collected, display the list of words again. Then have each student, in turn, silently display the contents of her bag. If the class correctly identifies the homograph in three guesses or less, circle that word on the chart. At the end of the activity, count the circled words. If there are more circled words than uncircled ones, reward students with a small treat or privilege.

bit, bow, dove, fair, fan, grave, hair, hide, lead, letter, litter, mole, object, peel, peep, pen, pool, register, resume, rich, roll, ruler, sign, sow, spring, switch, wave

Angel or Angle?

Using the correct word

Stamp out confusion over which word to use with this activity. Make a copy of the word cards below. Cut the cards apart and place them in a container. Have each child draw a word card; then let him find the classmate who is holding the word that is easily confused with his. Next, give each twosome two sheets of construction paper and two self-sticking labels. Have the pair label each sheet of paper with one of its words, a sentence that uses it correctly, and an illustration of the sentence. On each label, have the twosome copy one of its sentences and underline the easily confused word.

After everyone has finished, let each pair share its posters. Then collect the labels and affix them to several sheets of duplicating paper—placing each pair of easily confused words side by side—to create a study guide. Make a copy for each student; then punch holes in the copies so students can keep them in their notebooks as a ready reference.

Word Cards
Use with "Angel or Angle?" above.

accept	except	quite	quiet
angel	angle	conscience	conscious
breath	breathe	all ready	already
desert	dessert	capital	capitol
aisle	isle	stationery	stationary
lay	lie	aid	aide
lose	loose	sight	site
set	sit	principle	principal

Name _____

Let's Chat!

Directions: The following chat room conversation contains ten double negatives. Read the conversation and underline each sentence that contains a double negative. Below the screen, rewrite each sentence correctly. Use the back of this page if you need more space.

Example: He can't finish no homework tonight.
Corrections: He can finish no homework tonight.
He can't finish any homework tonight.

Sue: Hi, Bill!
Bill: Hi, Sue. How are you?
Sue: Well, okay, except my cat ran away again.
Bill: Haven't you never looked for her?
Sue: Yes, but I can't never seem to find Tiger when she runs off.
Bill: You should make posters of her.
Sue: I don't have no pictures of her.
Bill: I haven't never known anyone who doesn't have pictures of her pet.
Sue: Wait! I think my sister, Karen, took a picture of Tiger. I'll ask her.
Bill: Good idea! Is she going to Amy and Lisa's birthday party this Saturday?
Sue: Well, she doesn't have nothing to do on Saturday. I'll ask her.
Bill: Why don't Amy and Lisa never invite her to their parties?
Sue: Well, she wasn't never good friends with them.
Bill: I can't never think of a good gift for Amy or Lisa.
Sue: Me either! I don't never know what those twins want.
Bill: Well, I have to run. My work isn't never going to get done if I sit here all day. Good luck with Tiger.
Sue: Thanks. See you Saturday!

Bonus Box: Write another example, with its corrections, similar to the ones above.

Really Wrong Signs

While driving through a new town recently, you noticed something was *really* wrong with the signs there.

Directions: On the back of this page or on your own paper, rewrite each sign correctly. Then color the sign. Look carefully—most of the signs include more than one mistake!

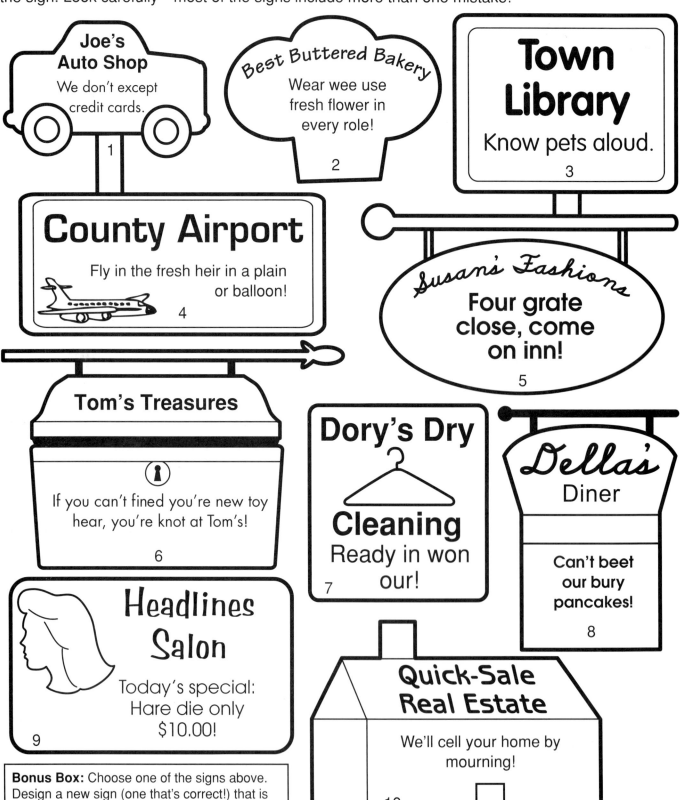

Joe's Auto Shop
We don't except credit cards.
1

Best Buttered Bakery
Wear wee use fresh flower in every role!
2

Town Library
Know pets aloud.
3

County Airport
Fly in the fresh heir in a plain or balloon!
4

Susan's Fashions
Four grate close, come on inn!
5

Tom's Treasures
If you can't fined you're new toy hear, you're knot at Tom's!
6

Dory's Dry Cleaning
Ready in won our!
7

Della's Diner
Can't beet our bury pancakes!
8

Headlines Salon
Today's special: Hare die only $10.00!
9

Quick-Sale Real Estate
We'll cell your home by mourning!
10

Bonus Box: Choose one of the signs above. Design a new sign (one that's correct!) that is sure to grab a customer's attention.

Answer Keys

Page 10

Jigsaw Puzzle
1. teacher created
2. It was
3. pieces did lock
4. puzzles were sold

Frisbee®
1. People tossed
2. Walter Morrison made
3. disc was remade
4. Morrison named

Monopoly®
1. Charles Darrow created
2. Darrow asked
3. company sold
4. Charles Darrow became

Yo-Yo
1. yo-yo was
2. Donald Duncan saw
3. Duncan experimented
4. He sold

Page 11

Compound Subject: BLUE
- B Cheese and jelly make a funny-tasting sandwich.
- L Chester and Charity crawled through the tunnel.
- U Morning, noon, and night are fine times for a nap.
- E Chuckie's mom and dad told him to eat cheese instead of ice cream.

Compound Predicate: SWISS
- S The mice hurried and scurried away.
- W Charity stretched and yawned before her nap.
- I Tom's paw searched and searched for a mouse.
- S Chuckie ran and hid from Tom.
- S Charity ate and drank until she couldn't move.

Compound Subject & Predicate: BRIE
- B Tom and his buddy found and fixed a trap.
- R Chester and Chuckie ate cheese and drank milk.
- I Chuckie and Charity nibbled and swallowed the cheese.
- E The mice and their friends chuckled and laughed at the silly cat.

None of the above: MOUSE
- M That cheese looks so yummy!
- O Tom pounced on the toy mouse.
- U I see the cat!
- S Chester loves checkers.
- E This cheese is crumbly.

Page 13

1.	F	7.	G	13.	A
2.	E	8.	R	14.	F
3.	E	9.	E	15.	F
4.	D	10.	E	16.	L
5.	M	11.	N	17.	E
6.	E	12.	W	18.	S

Message: Feed me green waffles!

Page 19

1. *green*—What is our tee time?
2. *red*—This course opened three years ago.
3. *yellow*—Drive the golf cart for the first nine holes.
4. *green*—Can I borrow your putter?
5. *red*—We will have lunch in the clubhouse.
6. *blue*—That runaway golf cart is heading straight for us!
7. *yellow*—Give me your money so I can pay the greens fee.
8. *blue*—I just beat the course record!
9. *red*—The groundskeeper does an excellent job taking care of the course.
10. *green*—Did you buy new golf shoes?
11. *red*—We should be finished with the course before lunch.
12. *green*—Have you ever hit a ball in a lake or sand trap?
13. *red*—We will need to return to the clubhouse if it starts to storm.
14. *yellow*—Take your shot so we can move to the next hole.
15. *blue*—Wow, that was a super shot!
16. *green*—Do you want to go golfing again next Saturday?
17. *yellow*—Meet me here at 8:00.
18. *blue*—I shot a hole in one!

Page 26

1.	C	5.	X	9.	X	13.	X
2.	X	6.	S	10.	C	14.	S
3.	S	7.	C	11.	X	15.	C
4.	X	8.	S	12.	C	16.	X

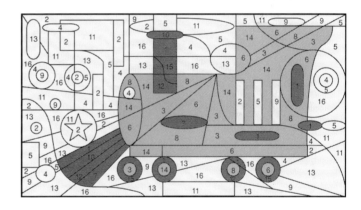

Page 32

Answers may vary slightly. Accept all reasonable answers.

1. The camp cook wanted to measure four ounces of syrup out of a jug. He had only a five-ounce and a three-ounce pitcher. How did he do it?

   Solution: The cook poured syrup from the jug into the three-ounce pitcher, then transferred these three ounces to the five-ounce pitcher. He then filled the three-ounce pitcher again and filled the five-ounce pitcher with two more ounces, leaving one ounce leftover in the three-ounce pitcher. Then he poured the five ounces from the five-ounce pitcher back into the jug. He poured the leftover ounce from the three-ounce pitcher into the five-ounce pitcher, then refilled the three-ounce pitcher with syrup. He added these ounces to the one ounce in the five-ounce pitcher, making four ounces!

Answer Keys

2. A sudden thunderstorm overturned a canoe. A girl swam to a rocky island. She rested in a deserted hut. She found an old kerosene lamp and a few matches. The wood on the island was too wet to build a fire. The lamp was her only way to signal for help. But the lamp held only an inch of kerosene and that wasn't enough to reach the lamp's short wick. How did she get the lamp to burn so she could signal for help?
    Solution: The girl dropped some small rocks she found on the rocky island in the lamp, raising the level of the kerosene so it would reach the wick.

3. The electricity was off in a boy's bedroom. He needed to find a clean pair of socks. His socks were all exactly alike except that half were black and half were brown. How many socks does he have to pull out before he is sure of getting a matched pair?
    Solution: If there are only two styles, the boy will only have to pull out three socks before making a matching pair.

4. A square house has four walls. Each wall has a window and each window faces the south. A bear walks by the window. What color is the bear?
    Solution: White. If all the windows are facing south, the house is at the North Pole. Therefore, the bear will be a polar bear.

5. A deep-sea fishing boat is docked in a harbor. A rope ladder hangs over the boat's side. The end of the ladder is just touching the water. The rungs of the ladder are one foot apart. The tide is rising eight inches an hour. How many rungs will be covered by water in two hours?
    Solution: None. The boat—and the ladder—will rise with the tide.

Page 39

1.	b	6.	a	11.	b
2.	a	7.	a	12.	a
3.	a	8.	a	13.	a
4.	b	9.	b	14.	b
5.	a	10.	b	15.	b

The bears are at Bumper's Pond.

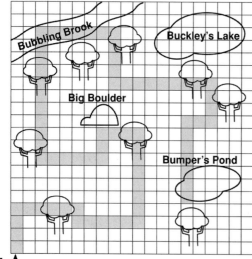

START

48

Page 40

1.	Nobody has	9.	No one joins
2.	Several have	10.	All...is
3.	Some...are	11.	...everyone hears
4.	Everyone is	12.	Several...look
5.	Nothing is	13.	Each...gazes
6.	Everything is	14.	Someone says
7.	Few...doubt	15.	Everyone puts
8.	Anyone is		

Page 45

Two corrections are given for each double negative.

1. **Bill:** Haven't you never looked for her?
    Have you never looked for her?
    Haven't you ever looked for her?
2. **Sue:** Yes, but I can't never seem to find Tiger when she runs off.
    Yes, but I can never seem to find Tiger when she runs off.
    Yes, but I can't ever seem to find Tiger when she runs off.
3. **Sue:** I don't have no pictures of her.
    I don't have any pictures of her.
    I have no pictures of her.
4. **Bill:** I haven't never known anyone who doesn't have pictures of her pet.
    I have never known anyone who doesn't have pictures of her pet.
    I haven't ever known anyone who doesn't have pictures of her pet.
5. **Sue:** Well, she doesn't have nothing to do on Saturday.
    Well, she doesn't have anything to do on Saturday.
    Well, she has nothing to do on Saturday.
6. **Bill:** Why don't Amy and Lisa never invite her to their parties?
    Why don't Amy and Lisa ever invite her to their parties?
    Why do Amy and Lisa never invite her to their parties?
7. **Sue:** Well, she wasn't never good friends with them.
    Well, she was never good friends with them.
    Well, she wasn't ever good friends with them.
8. **Bill:** I can't never think of a good gift for Amy or Lisa.
    I can never think of a good gift for Amy or Lisa.
    I can't ever think of a good gift for Amy or Lisa.
9. **Sue:** I don't never know what those twins want.
    I don't ever know what those twins want.
    I never know what those twins want.
10. **Bill:** My work isn't never going to get done if I sit here all day.
    My work isn't ever going to get done if I sit here all day.
    My work is never going to get done if I sit here all day.

Page 46

1. We don't <u>accept</u> credit cards.
2. <u>Where</u> <u>we</u> use fresh <u>flour</u> in every <u>roll</u>!
3. <u>No</u> pets <u>allowed</u>.
4. Fly in the fresh <u>air</u> in a <u>plane</u> or balloon!
5. <u>For</u> <u>great</u> <u>clothes</u>, come on <u>in</u>!
6. If you can't <u>find</u> <u>your</u> new toy <u>here</u>, you're <u>not</u> at Tom's!
7. Ready in <u>one</u> <u>hour</u>!
8. Can't <u>beat</u> our <u>berry</u> pancakes.
9. Today's special: <u>Hair</u> <u>dye</u> only $10.00!
10. We'll <u>sell</u> your home by <u>morning</u>!

Bonus Box answer: Students' signs will vary.